'Like many others before him, Loydell finds personal tragedy a galvanising force. His memorial work "Not My Dad Anymore" transcends everything else he has done.'
New Welsh Review

'a sequence of poems to his father that punches to the heart of loss and faith.'
Envoi

'Loydell sings his life, indeed revels in it. The downside of his awareness of mortality/vivacity comes with the atypically lengthy, typically touching memorial to his late father, "Not My Dad Anymore" - a series of vignettes evoking regret, familial frustration and loss with the simplest mutters. Resolutely simple and direct, Loydell's language resonates because he deals in identifiable-with emotions/scenarios, plainly yet poetically.'
Event South West

'One of the finest achievements of Loydell's poetry is that, somehow or other, it combines a sense of the personal with its exact opposite, which I suppose is the impersonal, objective, and in poetic terms a concern with language, and what innovation and risk in its use have revealed as possibilities. There is a profound sense of thought, humanity and caring here that is, to be frank, somewhat astonishing in that one doesn't come across it very often.'
Exultations and Difficulties

'There is a craft and style to Loydell's work which appeals to the orderly side of my brain. I like the way his mind plays with words and images. Again and again he uses the unexpected to illumine and define. What Loydell has produced is a balanced and beautifully stylistic display of great talent.'
Black Mountain Review

Other books by Rupert M Loydell include:

Poetry

> *A Conference of Voices*
> *Familiar Territory*
> *Endlessly Divisible*
> *The Museum of Light*
> *Home All Along*
> *Frosted Light: fourteen sequences*
> *The Giving Of Flowers*
> *Timbers Across The Sun*
> *Between Dark Dreams*

Prose

> *Stone Angels: Prose 1979-1993*

Collaborations

> *Snowshoes Across the Clouds* [with Robert Garlitz]
> *Eight Excursions* [with David Kennedy]
> *The Temperature of Recall* [with Sheila E. Murphy]
> *A Hawk into Everywhere* [with Roselle Angwin

The Smallest Deaths

Rupert M Loydell

Published by bluechrome publishing 2006

2 4 6 8 10 9 7 5 3 1

First published in Great Britain in 2006 by
bluechrome publishing
PO Box 109,
Portishead, Bristol. BS20 7ZJ

www.bluechrome.co.uk

A CIP catalogue record for this book is available from the British Library

ISBN   1-904781-90-X

Cover Photograph © Rupert M Loydell

The Smallest Deaths

Acknowledgements

These poems were first published in *Acumen, Ars-Interpres, Between Dark Dreams* [Acumen Publications, 1992], *Billy Jenkins. Entertainment USA: The Poems* [Stride Publications, 1995], *Blue Cage, Breathe, Coffeehouse, Communiqué, A Conference of Voices* [Shearsman Books, 2004], *Emotional Geology: the writings of Brian Louis Pearce* [Stride Publications, 1993], *Familiar Territory* [bluechrome publishing 2004], *Fill These Days* [Stride Publications, 1990], *Freedom is a Dangerous World* [Amnesty International, 1995], *Full of Star's Dreaming: Peter Redgrove 1932-2003* [Stride Publications, 2003], *The Gift* [Stride Publications, 2002], *Headlock, Keeping Faith* [The Spire Trust, 2004], *Litter*, The Matthew's House Project website, *The Merton Journal*, Moving Stories website [National Railway Museum, York], *My Kind of Angel. i.m. William Burroughs* [Stride Publications, 1998], *Oasis, Odyssey, Places We'll Never Get To* [Headlock Press, 1996], *Poethia, Poetry Review, Popularity Contest, Robert Lax: Speaking into Silence* [Stride Publications, 2003], *The Salzburg Review, Scratch, Shearsman, Stride, Surface, Timbers Across the Sun* [University of Salzburg, 1993], *Trajectories* [Phlebas, 1995], *Vallum.*

In 'Close the Door on Glory' the line 'the god of footprints accepts no prayers' is taken from Catherine Bennett's poem 'Refusal', in her book *Into Perfect Spheres Such Holes are Pierced.*

'Rats to the Stars/Telescope Eyes' was commissioned for the first Bath Literature Festival, and was broadcast on BBC Radio 3, accompanied by the music of Billy Jenkins.

Thanks to Brian Louis Pearce and Jane Routh for help with this collection.

Contents

The Smallest Deaths

Somehow
the smallest deaths
are the worst

The quiet
anulling
of memory

I scrabble
to place myself
in the picture

Not My Dad Anymore

I once heard a woman speak of her loneliness
as if it were a small bird. Imagine: her sorrow

had a wingspan!

- Olena Kalytiak Davis,
  'Should One Prefer Purity to Intensity of Soul?'

Not My Dad Anymore

I

Reduced to shit and sweat
and stretched skin
laid on a bed

your talk fades into
a blank gaze.
You're not my Dad anymore.

I still can't tell you
that I love you
in this grey unfriendly room.

Seems a matter of waiting
and I don't know whether to hope
or give up –

pray for an end
or a healing.
Miracles seem unlikely.

I'm crying
for myself it seems
or Mum, not you.

You're so bloody quiet
(never been a fighter) –
still in calm control.

You make sure we hear
that you're not in pain,
and that we shouldn't worry.

Of course we're worried!
Part of our life is lost –
you're missed already

we hurt, and we're afraid
of a future
that's going to change.

II

We're a million miles
away from
your grey room

rushing towards home
in the
late evening sun.

I think of you
drifting –
long hospice days

waiting for your
life
to crash land.

III

Back home
there's the usual pile of post
four hungry cats

messages on the ansaphone
and boxes of new books
to keep me busy

but I jump at the phone's ring
imagining
the finality that must come.

Difficult to feel
the same pain
across two hundred miles:

the stark reality
of you dying
has blurred.

I'm used to you
not being here
since I've left home
and intellectual
acceptance
doesn't make me cry

like waiting
to say goodbye
does...

I only wanted
you to know
that I was there

but you were dreaming
of a painless day –
healed and held –

as we wept and talked
across the bed
nervous and unsure.

IV

Sorting through my father's dreams
– boxes of model railway in the loft

his father's salvaged papers
and packages of photos and old books –

becomes confused with furnishings
earmarked for my sister's flat.

Everything's awry and in the wrong place.
There are no reasons for what's happened

all is higgledy-piggledy, we're confused
as we fill sacks, throw boxes down.

Heavier than we thought, more of it too.
Too much to let go of so soon.

Heavier than we thought
this burden of memory.

V

At least
two poets at the funeral

where the preacher said
how you were constant
and sure in your faith.

We're not
so convinced

both of us
can only wonder
and try to understand.

You
knew him as a friend

said how supportive he was
even when he didn't
fully understand your work.

I'm
a typical son

not felt close for years
now full of regrets
for things that I can't change.

Now
I'm left here

attempting
to get to grips
with death and words

still
trying

to cling
to what
he taught me.

Whilst
you're out and about

flogging
your new book
with childlike enthusiasm

happy
at how it's turned out.

Wishing
like me I suppose
it hadn't happened

quite
the way it did

perhaps
not so soon
even not at all.

Both struggling
to make some sense of it

glad we confided
in the face
of funereal certainty

sorry
we aren't so sure.

Caught in a place
where doubt
and question rule

and belief
is an optimistic don't know.

VI

Dad, I just wanted

you to know we were there
the day we drove back home.

I'd cried again
at the state you were in

– worse than the day before –
but thought the tears had dried.

Having to leave
without you knowing I'd been

was awful, reversed the flow.
I kept calling to you, hoping...

just wanted
to say goodbye Dad.

Goodbye.

Off-Balance

Half asleep
you tell me
I don't care
that Dad's dead.

You can't see
I'm living
with ghosts,
that I'm

still off-balance,
easily upset,
often caught
staring into space –

wondering how it is
one moment
someone is there,
and then not.

Like a Tombstone

'Language is how ghosts enter the world'
  – Anne Michaels, 'What the Light Teaches'

She decided to miss him;
that she wanted his name
spoken aloud, kept in use,
hung in the air, big and heavy,
often unwanted but always *there*.

Definitely *there*, as language,
not memory. Others were not
to be scared of mentioning him
now that he'd gone. Only later
did she stop and understand

that what they had named
was nostalgia's sleight of hand:
dust trapped in bright sunlight,
something not quite seen
out of the corner of your eye.

National Railway Museum

I am shadowing
the possibility
of your ghost
in the engine house
I never would have visited
were you here.

I look as though with you –
locos, carriages and models;
breathe in the smuts
of a hundred yard journey
on a working tank engine;
both nostalgic and excited.

I look for you:
a son seeking a father
among the iron facts
of the displayed past.
All steamed up
over nothing.

Tangerine Dream

for Dad

As synthesizers conjure musical space
I remember how this intrigued you most
out of all the music I played you as a boy.

You were fascinated by the abstraction,
the loops and echoes of new sounds
layered across rhythm and pulse.

You said it reminded you of a film you'd seen:
Scott of the Antarctic; and I, having always
been fascinated by the race to the Pole, concurred.

You didn't race for death, it took a little time.
But beside me in this icy emptiness
I remember your tilted head, you listening awhile.

(An eternity away, I sense you smile.)

Timbers Across the Sun

What a week! First
a friend dies, then it's
a weird kind of flu that
numbs and stiffens joints,
lays us out flat in bed –
useless for a day or two.

Then a couple call
to view the house again
and it seems that maybe
they'll buy. It looks different
in daylight, they say; we'll be
hearing from them soon.

But the place we want's gone,
and we're wondering whether
we want to leave here at all.
We're just getting used to
the new houses built opposite,
to having no view of the hills.

You can't argue can you?
I mean a deal's a deal, and you've
got to keep moving, you've got
to aim for the top. I think of your death
as, over the road, a man on the roof
nails timbers across the sun.

Lost

Low cloud.
Muffled stars
lost in the
warm beige sky.

The dying man
on TV
reminded me
of you.

You're lost
to me now.
I'm bathed
in starlight.

Year End

World darkens
with father's loss

(moss on ageing tree)

Meant the world
to me

Burning

Almost a year ago now that you left us,
and today the news of Francis Bacon's death
reminds me of your stay in the hospice,
how like his paintings you looked.
It's taken so long to miss you,
longer to stop the hurt that surprises.

The wind's howling outside,
and I've struggled to write of the artist,
of how his paintings move me.
Fashionable now to label his works
'horrific', but he clearly said
he just painted life the way that he saw it.

Both bohemian and nihilist,
but somehow telling awful truths
about how we've lost our way,
about power and lust and hate,
that awful *nothingness*
that most of us just drift through.

My father's the only person I've ever known
so sure about salvation, so *assured*.
We're far too full of the joys of life,
or worried and scared as we run about.
We're simply smears of dark pigment,
but Francis, Dad, you both burned bright.

The Memorial Stone

Here he comes the boy who tried to vanish to another time
is no longer with us with his sad blue eyes

Who will remember him?

– Brian Eno, 'Here He Comes'

Elegy

Another friend dead.
Been a bad year.

Seems hardly anyone
makes it through.

There's no song, no words
left in me today.

•

In the cathedral

religion sings to itself
an evensong.

Outside, the world wears spring
like a teenage girl struggling

to bear the weight of new breasts,
aghast at the interest they cause.

Sunshine
is no defence today.

The world's emptier
and more miserable than before.

I come home
to unwanted possessions

in the silver dark.

•

*The world's much lighter
maybe moving faster*

*but I wish it wasn't you
fell overboard.*

The Rest of the Space is Dark

i.m. Tony Charles

You simply do not know
who will become invisible

or a silence on the phone:
just a memory, someone gone.

We talked a lot about everything
except this final act.

•

There are always clouds outside
the windows at funerals,

always crowds of strangers
who knew the deceased better

and a huddle of others adrift,
awkward at the edge of things.

•

You will always be
asking for the bus to China,

kicking a five-a-side football,
and wanting another pint or two;

are still refusing the god
and his idea of self.

•

The clouds fuzz the window pane grey,
the wind cannot push them along.

Inside the school hall a
man improvises jazz in your name

and the sky clears a little,
allowing the puddles to shine.

His Own Words

for Peter Redgrove

'I can hear the wind in your voice'
   – Townes van Zandt to Jimmie Dale Gilmore

Whatever was before
the texts are texts are broken up
broken up into before

Someone made words made all these words
keep it you keep it remember the words
remind us what is there

A figure alone figure in a landscape
figure become landscape a landscape a country
hot rock from down below

Dark night island sparkle of darkness
moonlight glint flash flesh glint and sparkle
a fish beneath the waves

Light on water light on water
whisper of wind whisper of wind whisper in the trees
asleep and listening

The suggestion of birds some flying birds
flying through night throughout the night
the air is never still

Gradually drift gradual meaning
drift toward meaning drift toward stories
wanting to be told

Each time words each time the words
not quite the words not quite the same
each word full of voices

Dry cold paint cracked cold paint
people in pictures in pictures and paintings
other lives long gone

Most of the canvas the canvas is empty
bright amongst whiteness the emptiness white
all brightness fizz and fuss

Whatever was pictured those pictures
texture and stillness still something missing
a way of being alive

We have to find out we must find out
for ourselves in ourselves we have to find out
so many places to see

You struggle with struggle to define
filter what's seen filter vision memory
watch the storm outside

Attempt to pick up pick up what is
is out of reach stretch up reach out
learn to catch the breeze

Sudden attempt suddenly caught
broken up before being into before being
suddenly sunlight spills out

Consider the light admire the light
the way the light falls the shadows fall the way
shadows fill the room

His own work all his own work
out of words out of whatever whatever was before
the texts the texts are broken up

Rub clear the memorial stone

Other Rooms

i.m. Peter Redgrove

Full moon, high tide,
smell of salt in the air;
oceans can seem kind
but a man got washed away.

Windows emit more light
than pale sun gives out:
this was the house
of the laborator.

He owned
a collection of hills,
the secrets of pools,
rich smells and clay ooze.

What he knew
could only be said
in the language of thunder,
seen in sand and stone.

Departing from us
he left books of wisdom
and magic in the world;
many words of blessing.

The future's full of stories
and other rooms, unexplored.
They are in a different country
where we have no choice but to go.

Absence marks the opening of days,
loss grows fainter as the wind
tears his voice away. It is only
truly dark within the cave of self.

Love Letters on the Grave

i.m. Jim Morrison

Alert to nuances of mood and gesture,
to surfaces and the charm of accident,
oblivious to his own complexities,
he was the king who had been exiled,
set adrift in a series of dream events.

He knew magic when it happened.

Freed from time and other fundamentals,
the word webs he spun dazzle all of us,
his fictions masquerade as recorded facts.
He made music unique to this place,
had access to the realm of the sacred.

He knew how to make magic happen.

Men are not sounds, nor sounds men:
he spoke his lines and created theatre,
made it hard to ignore his presence,
or the silence as complete as darkness
when he fell over into paradise.

We know magic when it happens.

'I Am No Longer Who I Wasn't'

for David Michael / i.m. David Tibet

Manic ventriloquism, eloquent despair
and deception filled the imagination:

fault lines, key markers, polarities
everywhere, broken and spinning.

After the sound of a door creaking,
a quiet voice in the distant wind,

a man walking away from himself,
faint silhouette against the snow.

New life, new name, new beginning;
he has always been looking for this.

In the brilliant distance there is no dark,
only a clearing full of pure white light.

Undecided

i.m. Ken Smith

Highlight this:
time doesn't happen.
The language sees to that.

I'd like to live the quiet dream,
the quiet and space and order dream,
the white box in the city dream.

There's a breeze this morning
and the temperature's down.
I smell like myself again.

Is that enough certainty for today?
It's all I ever knew or had.
I was working out the implications.

But you? You'll never be sure.

Igloo

i.m. Robert Lax

Inside becomes outside; it is as grey
as day can be and as light as night
often is, depending on the season
and how wide your eyes are open.

It is dark outside now Robert
is no longer here. Words splinter
until we learn to read them,
islands of shadow on the page.

No escaping from or shelter in
the cold igloo we call death:
corridors of glass and snow,
stone memories pegged in place.

Outside seeps inside; it is as light
as it will ever be. You've slipped
away and I will never visit.
How wide-eyed alive you seem.

Close The Door On Glory

i.m. Agnes Martin

bright light   earth tones   clean air
vast open spaces of rows and lines

no objects disturb the horizon

a grid drawn on the page
turned out to be sublime

one-sided conversations
spoken in hidden pastels

twilight browns and greys

a line biroed on her hand
turned out to be love

a short whitewashed figure
sits mute on a stone bench

listening to the brushstroke wind

the god of footprints accepts no prayers
walks away from the landscape unseen

For Derek Jarman

absolute England
in love with delight
our gayest film-maker
who lost his sight
> *bone queer*
> *pearl child*

sweated propaganda
dark religious might
visual sensation
queenly delight
> *star struck*
> *super eight*

graffiti painter
of sexual heights
flickering candles
colour the night
> *live life*
> *out loud*

sculptural beach-head
channels sea-light
sheds, windswept garden,
greys, black and white
> *driftwood*
> *salt lick*

virus-disabled
losing a fixed fight
blues for the public –
sad music in flight
> *lover*
> *depart*

My Kind of Angel

i.m. William Burroughs

Nothing is greater than the freedom of the writer
when process disconnects from the real world.

When venturing over unknown terrain
there may arise rapture and trances, dislocation;

moments of happiness, moments of perfection,
a release from this world to a higher plane.

We are now into advanced states of idiocy,
collective fantasies monumentalized in public,

but must resist the intoxicants of the day.
We have written too much, it seems to me.

So many authors, some with great grief,
have come back recycled to haunt us.

Some able to transcend time and place
bring back reports of the eternal,

others take emotional or mystical roads.
Such journeys are always problematic.

Enchantment must be accompanied by reason,
one must listen to the faint tattoo of language.

You were flustered or nervous, a visionary genius
whose creative works expanded human consciousness.

I saw you at noon, tongue hanging out and eyes unfocussed.
You are my kind of angel. An affirmation of self.

'Profoundly Optimistic About Nothing'

'I have made images that the intellect
could never make...'
  – Francis Bacon (d. 28 April 1992)

Stretched forms
on sheets
of colour

sliding skin
at war
with itself

tensed
on arc
of bone

seated
awkwardly
on muscle

wrapped
in furniture
that frames

caught
in cages
empty rooms

where
windows show
shadowed vistas

ragged
and rubbed
to canvas edge

•

Optimistic about nothing
but captive to what
you alone find sensual:

x-rays
of the skull

the mouth
screaming pain

'the almost *Turneresque* colours'
of swollen lips and choking tongue

wrestlers
frozen mid-fall

lovers coupling
burning up flesh

your puffed face
in the mirror...

Skin on
skin on
mottled skin!

Oh! The beauty
of distress

the seduction
of disease

the kiss
of alcohol and paint

your endless empty life
finally cut short today

•

Drunk and heavy-jowled
you faced the future
with slurred optimism
paintbrush in hand

willing to gamble
on stain and smear –
the scraped worked paint
on reversed canvas

the throw of dice on baize
racehorses' straining necks
closing on the winning-post
The generosity of time

•

Self-portrait
survives

Heads
still scream

crucified
on gallery walls

but now
you are
only

an obituary
from the paper

a price
at auction

a painter
we knew of

a gambler
who won

a gambler
who finally lost

•

Today
you are
simply

meat
hung on
a hook

Ventriloquist

You've put my life into empty boxes:
each a set of records and tapes by
our many different bands,
along with photos and reviews.

You don't ever listen to our past.
The time for songs has gone
and even I am silent in my box:

giftwrapped for God
in best suit and shoes,
make-up on my face.

Don't bury yourself with me,
neither past nor future dreams
should be stacked away like this.

Memories won't be hidden,
and the children will want to see.
I know I've left the stage,
but please remember me.

Scotoma

for Fairnic again

Short term memory loss, flickering vision,
a headache to die for and sinuses aflame:
my punishment for believing in beer.

Dead seven years, but you won't stay away.
Someone who used to live nearby knew you,
and straightaway mentioned your name.

Nostalgia explodes or fires back in your face
when not used correctly. Pain is emphasised
if you grieve too long or linger in the past.

New life stirs as the dead come before
the most abstract of forms. Complex narratives
are reduced to simple emotional states,

doubts are brushed away, viewpoints and voices
made redundant; there is no argument anymore.
Just the words and skills you learned so well

finally put to use. Music and painting, laughter,
the art of great ideas: this is the language of heaven,
where colour exists in the present tense

and breathing is slowed only to waiting.
Transformed from temporal to eternal
all must face the silent text of actions.

In my bedroom a big pile of unread books,
and a television turned toward the window
in case the world outside is watching.

That which is elusive is now strangely present:
your animated liveliness dimly visible within this
hesitant nerd diagram, these awfully useless words.

Posthumous

He was a good man but let's not
make this an obituary just because
I should have written one before.

Don't ask me why I'm writing now
or why I'm not coherent. What he
meant to me is unspeakable, far more

than this blood wrung from a stone.
He was like sculpted rock, boulders
assembled precariously on the seashore.

Time tells us he married and had two
wonderful children. It also tells us
he's not with them now, not any more.

He didn't let us know him, did not
want any help, or us to share his life;
nor whatever is ahead or went before.

How Much Dying

It used to take a day to get there
for our fortnight holiday. Now,
we drive down in under an hour
every time there's another funeral.
Having gathered up all my poems
about death, here is another.

Philip says he has a video tape
of the afternoon and evening news
of 9/11. He's never watched it;
I want to, but don't know why.
How much dying there is all around.

Always unexpected, the news flash
that first alerts us to terrorist attack,
the phone call about somebody's death.
A firestorm of memory sweeps through
the building; tears can't put out flames.
I would have liked to say goodbye

but we're only distant family,
though close enough to visit.
Hymns and prayers are all we get,
eulogies and cups of tea, sandwiches,
brief words with cousins and strangers.

I'd prefer funerals to be miserable,
not a 'celebration of life'; want time
to mourn, some peace and quiet.
After the service your coffin's taken out
to the tune of 'What a Wonderful World'.
I try ever so hard to imagine it is.

Namesake

[How Much Dying 2]

My namesake killed himself with drink,
aunty had a massive stroke and died
just three weeks after burying uncle.

People disappear, lives change.
We no longer visit the places
where we have no reason to go.

If you don't travel there, then
memory goes away. Or fades,
like the photo beside our bed:

tin soldiers and model motorbikes
displayed behind your lovely smiles
in the house you had to move from.

Skirting depression's black hole
I long for childhood certainties,
time travel's impossible appeal.

But here we are in a small city
getting kids off to school in the rain,
trying to find time to be alive.

Further Than We Thought

We tried to make death look easy
as loss threaded through us.
Nothing, essentially, is forgotten
but silence is easier than memory.

Despite my faith in salvage
I will soon be running out of words.
We walked on the beach afterwards,
couldn't face the open grave.

Everyone was welcome back at the house,
so we went for tea and said goodbye.
It was further than we thought to home
and when we got there, difficult to stay.

What We Have Done

...he fears skinheads
in the drains and angels in the elevator

- Ken Smith, 'Message on the Machine'

What We Have Done

A man is trying to speak slowly and clearly,
struggling to pronounce his words just right.
He tells us how many bodies have been counted today.
In the background a bulldozer tips corpses into a pit

and a thin man with no shadow walks by.
He is not sure if he is happy to be alive.

The diver swims through oil and water,
fire and filth, desperate to stay alive.

I am building my own past from scratch;
the old one has gone up in smoke.

> A video loop is playing.
> The man on the screen starts to cry.

All this blue paint, all these burnt memories,
huge canvasses and smeared charcoal dust,
have not stopped the sun shining
or taken the tanks and bombs away.

Have not halted the bulldozer pushing corpses
or the man struggling to articulate hell.

> A video loop is playing.
> The man on the screen starts to cry.

The diver swims through oil and water,
fire and filth, desperate to stay alive.

He is a painted rock on a discovered tomb.
He is the past about to dive into a new moment.
He is trying to work out where he might be.
He is time trying to escape what we have done.

He is bobbing to the surface
not sure if he is happy to be alive.

Oil and water do not mix and the scars left,
the photos of this place, bear witness to this.

A video loop is playing.
The man on the screen starts to cry.

I am dying to tell you;
others simply died.

But there was nothing simple
about the way they died
and I am not sure any more
if I am happy to be alive

or if I would rather be diving into the black sea
and making my escape back to the familiar.

A video loop is playing.
The man on the screen starts to cry.

Rats to the Stars / Telescope Eyes

'...I and my fellow animal-creatures down here in the
swamp are as closely related to the extraterrestrials over
your heads as the rats to the stars and beyond...'
  – Dory Previn, *Bog-Trotter*

Charred remains twist,
higgledy-piggledy,
rustling cold in the grate.

Early morning wind,
that blew away the rain,
blows charcoal paper over.

Your face stares out
from the ash,
eyes a photocopy grey.

Burnt out poems,
rewritten songs
are gone...

•

The record clicks
over and over and over
needling your memory.

Somewhere in the street
someone is playing
your song.

Down here
in the swamp of the city
a guitarist – out of tune.

Down here
in the sunshine city
a madman – out of bounds.

The messages
are coming through
clear as day begins.

•

You are calm –
no more faces to burn
in those crystal eyes.

No more words
running around
looking for each other.

No more guitars
in your head
echoing in the distance.

•

Dawn stakes its claim
on the sky.

You are an upturned face
in a dim lit window

close to a place where
the bogeyman lives…

A shadow of yourself
that we have locked away.

•

You send letters
and write poems;
compose more songs:

lucid moments
in a galaxy
of madness –

your telescope eyes
two black holes
in space.

•

Music and graffiti. Blood-filled rooms.
Faded newsprint photos
stay frozen in the mind.

Sometimes there is madness in the air,
sometimes there are guitar sounds
needling the memory of the sunshine city.

Today a burst of static disrupts the music;
it ends with a gentle hiss of despair
and noise. Fading feedback. Silence.

Down here in the swamp of the city
the messages are coming through.
You're just a shadow of ourselves.

Heatwave (Scratching the Surface)

for Neil

Radiator grills and musical ghosts.
Skyscrapers reflect crazy paving,
grey wheels and grey windows,
paintings I don't like.
Secret surveillance missions
and flags get to me,
kind of stick in the mind.
This bookshop looks good.

That box of 9/11 dust
and shredded steel was scary;
everyone nearby
moved to somewhere else.
I'm not sure about
this weather, clear skies,
wet heat. Just feel the heat.
Put your camera away.

The hotel's cheap, my bag is full,
live music is the way to go.
The place I wanted to eat at
is closed, but the diner is open.
The circuit seems complete,
the PA booms announcements
of both arrivals and departures.
I suppose we shouldn't complain.

You only scratch the surface here
driving through the days, wandering
within the triangle of the Flat Iron.
I don't feel threatened anywhere
and the band we saw stagger out,
making up precise instructions,
went back the next day. It was worth it;
taxis are much cheaper than you think.

Trace our steps downtown,
the huge bulk starting to fade.
Paint the streets' secrets
wide open with the engine running.
Actually, that fence reminded me again:
cold war secrets not right to these eyes.
Stop and shoot another photo up there.
What is it about water towers?

Cold beer, cheese and tomato subs,
in dimlit bars are enough.
You sit in the shadow
with the Chrysler Building
somewhere up above us;
it is as you'd hoped. Pure warmth
won't fill you with a rosy glow,
the colours are too hit and miss.

An apex, a wedge, dividing the streets,
with a bar open right next door.
There are still records to be bought
before having an early drink or two.
I'm sorry I went the wrong way,
on the subway I simply get lost.
Today we are in full agreement;
voice and mood come together.

Forget the roof garden and its great view,
just look at the size of that building!
The sooty day is shimmering, hazy,
a monochrome blurred version
of those Joan Mitchell paintings
I wanted to meet. I'm glad
that we went up but now don't want
to go as high, am starting to fade.

This is difficult to write.
It has only been such a short time.
The tidy excavation downtown,
the chips and scars of buildings…
We must save something,
one perspex cube of debris.
Ominous, I reckon, that
END scrawled on the door.